T0365877

Nicholas D'Andrea, Jr.

We Meet Again

Reminiscing never felt so good

FIRST EDITION

To order additional copies of this book, contact:
Xlibris
844-714-8691
www.Xlibris.com
Orders@Xlibris.com

Poetry by Nicholas D'Andrea, Jr.
Photography by Rich Pomerantz
Illustrations by Michael Byrne

Published by Dark Horse Studio, Waterbury, CT

ISBN:	Softcover	978-1-4134-9001-5
	Hardcover	978-1-4134-9091-6
	EBook	978-1-6698-4867-7

Library of Congress Control Number: 2005902257

Print information available on the last page

Rev. date: 09/22/2022

Here's to the time-honored handshakes
that greet warm remembrance…

4

The Dream
1. We Meet Again (Somewhere in a Dream)
2. A Taste of August in Autumn
3. You
The Waves
4. From Forest to Beach
5. Homesick Tears
6. Nostalgia
7. Whistle in the Wind
8. My Childhood Days
9. You Are My Life
10. Single Whisper
The Touch
11. Imaginary Love Scenes
12. Ebony Dreams
13. Ancient Mist
14. The Quiet Square
15. As Our Lips Meet
The Eyes
16. In Your Garden
17. Shy Boy Lost in a Big Crowd
18. Winter Blue
19. In Late December Snow
20. Dawn Comes When the Sun Rises
21. With Innocence
The Path
22. Destiny
23. The Future Can't Replace the Past
24. Gravel Road
25. The Hollywood Song
26. Where Do We Go from Here?
27. It Hurts Too Much to Say Good-bye
28. After I'm Gone

The Dream

1. We Meet Again (Somewhere in a Dream)

The stars are crying tears tonight,
they are the raindrops that soak my pillow
where my head rests and dreams flow.

Soon your reflection appears,
so faint as it stares
into my closed eyes

and before they can open, you're gone.
It seemed so real –
Was it just a dream?

2. A Taste of August in Autumn

A strong breeze
holding hands
with rusty leaves,
fields of hay
by roads of
cobblestone grey,
apple pie
aroma,
and changing sky
all whisper
in my ear
about summer
raining heat
on pavement
under bare feet,
sun-filled days
and sandy walks
by ocean waves,
it's August
revisited!

3. You

Your perfume,
            carried on a misty breeze,
            envelops me;
            its airborne scent
            was meant
            to please.

Your eyes,

            glistening a stunning hue
            of baby blue,
            simply draw me
            right into you.

Your hair,

            a flowing stream of satin
            shining flaxen,
            could never grow coarse
            or blacken.

Your touch,

            as soft as a newborn rose
            and satin bows,
            is gentle like
            the breeze that blows.

The Waves

4. From Forest to Beach

In search of a little love and romance,
I eagerly consume your seductive glance
As if it were a piece of dark sweet chocolate.

Your soft figure sways like a wind-blown tree,
Stretching its branches out to embrace me
With a grip like no elm or maple I know.

Soon the scene changes from forest to beach,
You are smooth driftwood floating within reach
Of hot sand that begs for thirst-quenching water.

Waves in a symphony crashing 'pon shore
Retreat momentarily and come back for more,
Their lust for the sand's heat too great to resist.

With quickest speed the crescendos subside,
Reaching their climax they fade out with the tide
As the sun strokes the evening's pink horizon.

5. Homesick Tears

Homesick tears
            are drops in a waterfall glistening
            where summer heat abounds
            and the youthful evening
            squanders, upon warm grounds,
            its precious moonbeams.
Sunfast dreams
            are sleepless ocean waves traveling
            from calm night to boist'rous day
            without ever stopping
            for anything in their way
            until shore they meet.
Inner peace
            is quietude overshadowing
            dormant seeds that will yield
            erotic flowers blooming
            in a passionate field
            of tranquility.

6. Nostalgia

The shoreline disappears
Beneath the white foam,
As the pink sky clears
Where wispy clouds roam;
I forget all my fears
When I am alone,
But it's nice to hear
Someone call me home

7. Whistle in the Wind

The wind styles my hair
in the strangest ways,
as it scurries through
the October haze.

I labor to walk,
stumbling too often;
the force weighs me down
on roads that I'm crossin'

But not far away
I hear a faint tune
guiding me homeward
beneath the grey moon.

8. My Childhood Days

    Happy memories
        let me drift away
        on the peaceful seas
        of my childhood days,

    My soul is soothed
        by temperate waves
        and my mind is moved
        by the dreams it saves,

    Faces of long ago
        cast smiles back at me
        where these waters flow
        through eternity

9. You Are My Life

You are my fire
      in the dead of winter,
You are my light
      in the dead of night,
You are my savior
      in the face of despair,
You are my guide
      when I can't decide,
You are my friend
      to the very end,
You are the sunrise
      that clears cloudy skies,
You are the flower
      that feeds me sweet nectar,
You give me life,
      you are my life.

10. Single Whisper

Wishes and dreams
That never come true,
The feeling of being
Around without you,
A prayer to shout
But a voice never heard,
Echoes ring out
Not speaking a word.

My thoughts and dreams
So faithful and true,
Eternally seem
To revolve around you,
A prayer too soft
To even be heard,
Echoes die off
In search of a word.

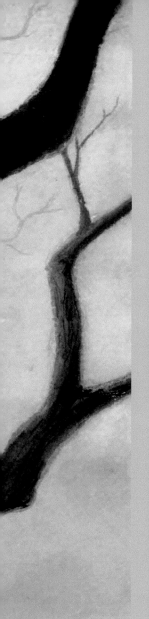

The Touch

11. Imaginary Love Scenes

I still don't know what it means
when rolling cameras capture
imaginary love scenes:

not a single soul stirs
deep in the heart of the woods
holding lakes that are mirrors

reflecting a sturdy view
of a solid form standing
in the dense brush before you

with your silky hair flowing
in the midst of summer rains
and the warmest winds blowing

on hidden parts now exposed
to the most intense sunlight
tearing through delicate clothes

that never let my eyes see
until the picture fades with
its life-giving fantasy.

Hmm…I must have run out of film.

12. Ebony Dreams

I search for a night
where the calm air meets
tender starlight
that caresses smooth streets
running through meadows
of ebony dreams
and holding shadows
cast by you and me.

13. Ancient Mist

Memories entangled in an ancient mist
      are hidden well from view,
I strain to remember what life was like
      before the day I met you:

      the laughter and tears,
      sweet dreams and nightmares,
      the hugs and kisses,
      hits or near misses,
      the late nights of fun
      and workdays of boredom.

The good things and bad things trapped in my past
      are simply one great blur,
I've given up trying to catch a glimpse
      since you entered the picture.

14. The Quiet Square

    Where we thought we lived
    The house is empty,
        The number on the door
        Isn't there anymore;
    Weeds have taken over
    The quiet square of land,
        And skies collide
        With time gone by.

15. As Our Lips Meet

I sense something strange
  as our lips meet,
  a taste so hot,
  so burning-sweet;
  with force so great
  yet pleasing touch
  we melt as one,
  desire too much

The Eyes

16. In Your Garden

In your garden
    I wish I could be,
    such a comforting place
    of tranquility…
Your violets,
    tiny and tender,
    cordially greet
    all who enter.
Your red roses,
    tainted with fragrance,
    capture my heart
    with pure elegance.
Your irises,
    squinting at sunlight,
    emerge from their sleep
    a breath-taking sight.
And your orchids,
    swelling with beauty,
    bear soft petals
    that gently soothe me.

17. Shy Boy Lost in a Big Crowd

Skyscrapers vaulting
    into off-blue,
Sidewalks stretching
    the city through,
Lost in my daydreams
    I bump into you,
Both our eyes meet:
    brown versus blue,
Words escape me
    and you offer few,
The crowd swallows me
    then you're missing, too.

18. Winter Blue

And then it happened…
A furious gust of wind
        cursed the lifeless trees,
Transforming them into
        a writhing mass of wood,
And only my heartache-filled soul
        could challenge the mighty harbinger of ice
        as it tinted the landscape
        with a shadow of blue.

19. In Late December Snow

A frigid hand grips
        the unwary being
Whose warm, rosy lips
        touch the deep wounds bleeding

The soft, breathless kiss
        fails to start the healing
When a sharp word slips
        on the truth revealing

It used to be shy
        so many years ago
Until its haunting cry
        demanded that we know

The white birch will try
        in late December snow
To conceal its sigh
        beneath loud winds that blow.

20. Dawn Comes When the Sun Rises

His soaring vocals
smother the weighty words
falling from her tongue,
a candle flame
flickering in the night;
with a look in his eyes
so penetrating
she submits willingly
and withdraws all fears.

A few heavy sighs
then escape in the heat
of the listless night,
like soft echoes
quivering at the sight
of gold chasing the east;
jilted once again,
the west makes no effort
to hold back its tears.

21. With Innocence

I break your hold
So weak and cold,
My thoughts are never told.

Your eyes pierce me
With innocence so sweet
I strain to keep
My tears from falling.

The Path

22. Destiny

Oh, little yellow leaf
Floating down the stream,
What things can you see
On your winding journey?

"Twigs, stones, and the trees
Dropping more colored leaves
Into this flowing stream
Searching for their destiny."

It's too bad that birds flying south
Cannot stop to talk right now,
For with their view they'd know how
Things downstream might all turn out.

So, good luck to you, little leaf
There's no need for you to worry,
Wherever you're pulled by the stream
You're sure to find your destiny.

23. The Future Can't Replace the Past

Many a night I used to cry –
I didn't know the reason why
I really wasn't satisfied
With all the years that had gone by.
A nice, long walk down roads that wind
Helped me think and clear my mind
To see I did enjoy those times
And miss the life I've left behind.

24. Gravel Road

Kicking stones
along the road,
    Plucking leaves
        from low-branched trees,
            Shading eyes
                from sunny skies,
Helping those
with many woes,
    Thinking of things
    that life brings,
        Being wise
        to realize:
I am just
a speck of dust
    In this perverse
    universe.

25. The Hollywood Song

You're in the spotlight once again,
How perfect you look standing there
Like a young flower under the sun,
You're in bloom everyday of the year.

Sometimes the sun takes you for a ride
On its glittering golden rays,
Just be careful – it's quite expensive
And may not be traveling both ways.

I'm sure that this won't dissuade you
Since you've made up your mind to go,
I guess it's time to say good-bye
To my little Marilyn Monroe.

26. Where Do We Go from Here?

Where do we go from here?
I do not know,
The path is no longer clear.

Put your soft hand in mine,
We'll go together
So that, even if we're lost,
We won't be alone.

Where do we go from here?
As long as we're together,
I guess it doesn't really matter.

27. It Hurts Too Much to Say Good-Bye

A salty tear
        Now leaves my eye,
                It hurts too much
                        To say good-bye.

I don't know when
        We'll meet again
                So please keep me
                        In memory.

28. After I'm Gone

Don't forget me
After I'm gone,
Let each memory
Sing its own song;
A new melody
Born each dawn
Shall give you strength
To carry on.

Printed in the United States
by Baker & Taylor Publisher Services